Attract
Happiness

Attract Happiness

Take Charge of Your Life

JOSEPH MURPHY

foreword by David Cameron Gikandi
author of *A Happy Pocket Full of Money*

Cover and text design by Kathryn Sky-Peck
Typeset in Centaur

Hampton Roads Publishing Company, Inc.
Charlottesville, VA 22906
Distributed by Red Wheel/Weiser, LLC
www.redwheelweiser.com

Sign up for our newsletter and special offers by going to
www.redwheelweiser.com/newsletter.

ISBN: 978-1-64297-032-6

Library of Congress Cataloging-in-Publication Data available upon request.

Printed in the United States of America
IBI

10 9 8 7 6 5 4 3 2 1

Contents

Foreword

The pursuit of happiness is known by every human being that has ever lived. We are designed to move away from pain and move toward pleasure, happiness. Just like breathing and drinking water, seeking happiness is intrinsic to the human condition. We're all driven by this irresistible urge.

Many of us spend a great deal of our lives seeking happiness in all the wrong places. Like trying to get blood from a stone, never fully grasping that we can't find what was never there. Perhaps the biggest obstacle is the belief that happiness comes from external conditions: "When my spouse changes, I will be happy." "When I make more money, I will be happy." "When the government cleans up its act, I will be happy."

Those under this spell find themselves unhappy much of the time because, the truth is, there will always be obstacles on our path. There will always be things outside of us that we can't control. Yet, happiness is literally at our fingertips.

Joseph Murphy was one of the most important New Thought teachers of the 20th century. He wrote, taught, and lectured widely on consciousness and human potential. His words show us that we can find joy in troubled times. Not only can you create and experience life more deliberately and bring about conditions that you prefer but also, even without those conditions, you can create happiness from within. Happiness is an inside job, and you have full freedom and control over it. You create happiness through the meaning and identity you attach to your thoughts and emotions—your subconscious. You may not always be able to control external events but you always have total control over how you approach them.

Attract Happiness reminds us of our true source of happiness, which occurs when we align our subconscious with the Source of Life within us, the Source from which all things flow—the power of Life. And it is within you. It expresses *as* you, *through* you, *for* you.

The world has taught us, over millennia, to turn away from our True Selves, to forget our own divine creative power, to think of ourselves as mere flesh and bones, as insignificant creatures at the mercy of external forces. A person who is unaware of their own inner spiritual powers falls subject to their fears, their conditioned and limiting thoughts and emotions, to mass unconsciousness. The person that has awakened to their relationship with Source becomes a conscious creator who keeps a steady internal compass despite what might be happening around them and in the world.

In my experience, all of humanity's problems have only one root cause: the deep-seated belief in the illusion of separation from Source. But in each moment, you can choose to align with Source, rather than with fear. This allegiance is expressed literally through your thoughts and emotions. By refusing to entertain self-defeating thoughts and emotions, you choose happiness.

Joseph Murphy's words will help you identify and strengthen your connection to the Source within you. Reading them will give you

There will always
be things outside
of us that we can't
control. Yet, happiness
is literally at our
fingertips.

increasing confidence in the belief that you can attract happiness. Take charge of your life. Claim your right to be unconditionally happy. Enjoy this little book.

—DAVID CAMERON GIKANDI,
author of *A Happy Pocket Full of Money*

Introduction

Everyone desires health, happiness, security, peace of mind, and true expression, but many fail to achieve clearly defined results. A university professor once admitted to me, "I know that if I changed my mental pattern and redirected my emotional life, my ulcers would not recur, but I do not have any technique, process, or *modus operandi*. My mind wanders back and forth on my many problems, and I feel frustrated, defeated, and unhappy."

This professor had a desire for perfect health; he needed knowledge of the way his mind worked, knowledge that would enable him to fulfill his desire. By practicing the methods outlined in this book, he became whole and found the happiness he sought.

Why is one person sad and another happy? Why are some joyous and prosperous and others poor and miserable? Why is one fearful and anxious and another full of faith and confidence? Why is it so many good, kind religious people suffer the tortures of the damned in their mind and body? Why is it many immoral and irreligious people succeed and prosper and enjoy abundance and happiness? Is there an answer to these questions in the workings of your conscious and subconscious minds?

There most certainly is.

It is for the express purpose of answering and clarifying these questions and many others of a similar nature that motivated me to write this book. I have endeavored to explain the great fundamental truths of your mind in the simplest language possible.

I believe that it is perfectly possible to explain the basic, foundational, and fundamental laws of life and of your mind in ordinary everyday language. I urge you to study this book and apply the techniques outlined herein; and as you do, I feel absolutely convinced that you will lay hold of a miracle-working power that will lift you up from confusion, misery, melancholy, and failure, and guide you to your true place, solve your difficulties, sever you from emotional and physical bondage, and place you on the royal road to freedom, peace of mind,

The miracle-working power of your subconscious mind can heal you of what is holding you back.

and happiness. This miracle-working power of your subconscious mind can heal you of what is holding you back, and help you learn to use your inner powers to open the prison door of fear and enter into a life described by Paul as the glorious liberty of the children of God.

The unique feature of this book is its down-to-earth practicality. Here you are presented with simple, usable techniques and formulas, which you can easily apply in your day-to-day world. I have taught these simple processes to men and women all over the world, to individuals from all walks of life, and presented this material to classes of more than a thousand men and women of all religious affiliations—many attendees came from distances of two hundred miles or more for each class lesson.

The special features of this book will appeal to you because they show you why oftentimes you get the opposite of what you prayed for and reveal to you the reasons why. People have asked me in all parts of the world and thousands of times, "Why is it I have prayed and prayed and got no answer?" In this book you will find the reasons for this common complaint. The many ways of impressing the subconscious mind and getting the right answers make this an extraordinarily valuable book and an ever-present help in a time of trouble.

WHAT DO YOU BELIEVE?

It is not the thing believed in that brings an answer to our prayer; the answer to prayer results when our subconscious mind responds to the mental picture or thought we have in mind. This law of belief is operating in all religions of the world and is the reason why they are psychologically true. Buddhists, Christians, Muslims, and

Jews all may get answers to their prayers, not because of the particular creed, religion, affiliation, ritual, ceremony, formula, liturgy, incantation, sacrifices, or offerings, but solely because of belief or mental acceptance and receptivity about that for which they pray.

The law of life is the law of belief, and belief could be summed up briefly as a thought in your mind. As you think, feel, and believe, so is the condition of your mind, body, and circumstances. A technique, a methodology based on an understanding of what you are doing and why you are doing it, will help you to bring about a subconscious embodiment of all the good things of life.

Essentially, answered prayer is the realization of your heart's desire.

Your prayer is answered because your subconscious mind is principle, and by principle I mean the way a thing works. For example, the principle of electricity is that it works from a higher to a lower potential. You do not change the principle of electricity when you use it, but by cooperating with nature, you can bring forth marvelous inventions and discoveries that bless humanity in countless ways.

Your subconscious mind is principle and works according to the law of belief. You must know what belief is, why it works, and how it works. The law of your mind is the law of belief. This means you must believe in the way your mind works in order to believe in belief itself. The *belief* of your mind is the *thought* of your mind—that is simple, just that and nothing else.

All your experiences, events, conditions, and acts are the reactions of your subconscious mind to your thoughts. Remember, it is not the thing

Understanding what you are
doing and why you are doing
it will help bring about a
subconscious embodiment of
all the good things of life.

believed in but the belief in your own mind that brings about the result.

Cease believing in the false beliefs, opinions, superstitions, and fears of mankind. Begin to believe in the eternal truths of life, which never change. Then, you will move onward, upward, and Godward.

The miracle-working powers of your subconscious mind existed before you and I were born, before any church or world existed. The great eternal truths and principles of life antedate all religions.

It is with these thoughts in mind that I urge you in the following chapters to lay hold of this wonderful, magical, transforming power, a power that will bind up mental and physical wounds, proclaim liberty to the fear-ridden mind, and liberate you completely from the limitations of unhappiness, failure, misery, lack, and frustration. All you have to do is unite mentally and emotionally with the good you wish to embody, and the creative powers of your subconscious will respond accordingly.

Begin now, today, let wonders happen in your life!

chapter one

Meet Your
Subconscious Mind

You have only one mind but your mind possesses two distinctive characteristics. The line of demarcation between the two is well known to all thinking men and women today. The two functions of your mind are essentially unalike. Each is endowed with separate and distinct attributes and powers.

Your mind is a duality. The dual nomenclature generally used to distinguish the two functions of your mind is as follows: the objective and subjective mind, the conscious and subconscious mind, the waking and sleeping mind, the surface self and the deep self, the voluntary mind and the involuntary mind, the male and the female, and many other similar terms. Throughout this book, you will find the terms *conscious* and *subconscious* used to represent the dual nature of your mind.

THE CONSCIOUS AND SUBCONSCIOUS MINDS

An excellent way to get acquainted with the two functions of your mind is to look upon your own mind as a garden. You are a gardener, and you are planting seeds (thoughts) in your subconscious mind all day long, based on your habitual thinking. As you sow in your subconscious mind, so shall you reap in your body and environment.

Begin now to sow thoughts of peace, happiness, right action, good will, and prosperity. Think quietly and with interest on these qualities and accept them fully in your conscious reasoning mind. Continue to plant these wonderful seeds (thoughts) in the garden of your mind, and you will reap a glorious harvest, a harvest of happiness. Your subconscious mind may be likened to the soil, which will grow all kinds of seeds, good or bad. Do you gather grapes or thorns, figs or thistles? Every thought is, therefore, a cause, and every condition is an effect. For this reason, it is essential that you take charge of your thoughts so as to bring forth only desirable conditions.

When your mind thinks correctly, when you understand the truth, when the thoughts deposited in your subconscious mind are constructive, harmonious, and peaceful, the magic-working power of your subconscious will respond and bring about harmonious conditions, agreeable surroundings, and the best of everything.

When you begin to control your thought processes, you can apply the powers of your subconscious to any problem or difficulty. In other words, you will actually be consciously cooperating with the infinite power and omnipotent law, which governs all things.

Look around you wherever you live and you will notice that the vast majority of mankind lives in the *outer* world; the more enlightened people are intensely more interested in the world *within*. Remember, it is the inner world—namely, your thoughts, feelings, and imagery—that creates your outer world. It is, therefore, the *only* creative power, and everything that you find in your world of expression has been created by you in the inner world of your mind, consciously or unconsciously.

Knowledge of the interaction of your conscious and subconscious minds will enable you to transform your whole life. In order to change external conditions, you must change the cause. Most people try to change conditions and circumstances by working with conditions and circumstances. However, to remove discord, confusion, lack, and limitation you must remove the *cause*, and the cause is the way you are using your conscious mind. In other words, the way you are thinking and picturing in your mind.

You are living in a fathomless sea of infinite riches. Your subconscious is very sensitive to your thoughts. Your thoughts form the mold or matrix through which the infinite intelligence, wisdom, vital forces, and energies of your subconscious flow. The practical application of the laws of your mind as illustrated throughout this book will cause you to experience abundance for poverty, wisdom for superstition and ignorance, peace for pain, joy for sadness, light for darkness, harmony for discord, faith and confidence for fear, success for failure, and freedom from the law of averages. In a word, happiness.

Certainly, there can be no more wonderful blessing than these outcomes from a mental, emotional, and material standpoint. Most of the great scientists, artists, poets, singers, writers, and inventors have a deep understanding of the workings of the conscious and subconscious minds.

LITTLE ME, BIG ME

There is a story that at one time, Caruso, the great operatic tenor, was struck with stage fright. He said his throat was paralyzed due to spasms caused by intense fear, which constricted the muscles of his vocal chords. Perspiration poured copiously down his face. He was ashamed because in a few minutes he had to go out on the stage, yet he was shaking with fear and trepidation. He said, "They will laugh at me. I can't sing." Then, in the presence of those backstage with him, he shouted out, "The Little Me wants to strangle the Big Me within."

He said to the Little Me, "Get out of here, the Big Me wants to sing through me." By the Big Me, he meant the limitless power and wisdom of his subconscious mind, and he began to shout, "Get out, get out, the Big Me is going to sing!"

His subconscious mind responded, releasing the vital forces within him.

When the call came, he walked out on the stage and sang gloriously and majestically, enthralling the audience.

It is obvious that Caruso must have understood the two levels of mind—the conscious or rational level, and the subconscious or irrational level. Your subconscious mind is reactive and responds to the nature of your thoughts. When your conscious mind (the Little Me) is full of fear, worry, and anxiety, the negative emotions engendered in your subconscious mind (the Big Me) are released and flood the conscious mind with a sense of panic, foreboding, and despair. When this happens, you can, like Caruso, speak affirmatively and with a deep sense of authority to the irrational emotions generated in your deeper mind as follows: "Be still, be quiet, I am in control, you must obey me, you are subject to my command, you cannot intrude where you do not belong."

It is fascinating and intensely interesting to observe how you can speak authoritatively and

Happiness is
a state of
mind.

with conviction to the irrational movement of your deeper self, bringing silence, harmony, and peace to your mind. The subconscious is *subject* to the conscious mind, and that is why it is called subconscious or *subjective*.

The great secret possessed by great people throughout the ages was their ability to contact and release the powers of their subconscious mind—for abundance, for peace, for happiness. You can do the same.

chapter two

Happiness and
Your Subconscious Mind

William James, father of American psychology, said that the greatest discovery of the nineteenth century was not in the realm of physical science.

The greatest discovery was the power of the subconscious touched by faith.

In every human being is that limitless reservoir of power, which can overcome any problem in the world. True and lasting happiness will come into your life the day you get the clear realization that you can overcome any weakness—

the day you realize that your subconscious can solve your problems, heal your body, and prosper you beyond your fondest dreams.

You might have felt very happy when your child was born, when you got married, when you graduated from college, or when you won a great victory or a prize. You might have been very happy when you became engaged to the loveliest, most handsome life partner. You could go on and list innumerable experiences, all of which have made you happy.

However, no matter how marvelous these experiences are, they do not give real lasting happiness—they are transitory.

The Book of Proverbs gives the answer: *Whosoever trusteth in the Lord, happy is he.* When you trust in the Lord (the power and wisdom of your subconscious mind) to lead, guide, govern, and direct all your ways, you will become poised, serene, and relaxed. As you radiate love, peace, and good will to all, you are building a superstructure of happiness for all the days of your life.

YOU MUST CHOOSE HAPPINESS

Happiness is a state of mind. There is a phrase in the Bible that says, *Choose ye this day whom ye will serve.* You have the freedom to choose happiness. This may seem extraordinarily simple, and it is. Perhaps this is why people stumble over the way to happiness; they do not see the simplicity of the key to happiness. The great things of life are simple, dynamic, and creative. They produce well-being and happiness.

St. Paul reveals to you how you can think your way into a life of dynamic power and happiness in these words: *Finally, brethren, whatsoever things are true, whatsoever things are honest, whatsoever things are just, whatsoever things are pure, whatsoever*

As you radiate love,
peace, and good will to
all, you are building a
superstructure of happiness
for all the days of your life.

things are lovely, whatsoever things are of good report; if there be any virtue, and if there be any praise, think on these things. Philippians 4:8

HOW TO CHOOSE HAPPINESS

Begin now to choose happiness. This is how you do it: When you open your eyes in the morning, say to yourself, "Divine order takes charge of my life today and every day. All things work together for good for me today.

"This is a new and wonderful day for me. There will never be another day like this one. I am divinely guided all day long, and whatever I do will prosper.

"Divine love surrounds me, enfolds me, and envelops me, and I go forth in peace. Whenever my attention wanders away from that which is good and constructive, I will immediately bring it back to the contemplation of that which is

Thoughts repeated
regularly and
systematically sink into
the subconscious mind
and become habitual.
Happiness is a habit.

lovely and of good report. I am a spiritual and mental magnet attracting to myself all things that bless and prosper me. I am going to be a wonderful success in all my undertakings today. I am definitely going to be happy all day long."

Start each day in this manner; then you will be choosing happiness, and you will be a radiant joyous person.

MAKE IT A HABIT TO BE HAPPY

A number of years ago, I stayed for about a week in a farmer's house in Connemarra on the west coast of Ireland. He seemed to be always singing and whistling and was full of humor.

I asked him the secret of his happiness, and his reply was: "It is a habit of mine to be happy. Every morning when I awaken and every night before I go to sleep, I bless my family, the crops, the cattle, and I thank God for the wonderful harvest."

This farmer had made a practice of this for over forty years. As you know, thoughts repeated regularly and systematically sink into the subconscious mind and become habitual. He discovered that happiness is a habit.

YOU MUST DESIRE TO BE HAPPY

There is one very important point about being happy. You must sincerely desire to be happy. There are people who have been depressed, dejected, and unhappy for so long that if they were suddenly made happy by some wonderful, good, joyous news, they would actually be like the woman who said to me, "It is wrong to be so happy!" They have been so accustomed to the old mental patterns that they do not feel at home being happy! They long for the former, depressed, unhappy state.

Begin to realize
that the world you
live in is determined
largely by what goes
on in your mind.

I knew a woman in England who had rheumatism for many years. She would pat herself on the knee and say, "My rheumatism is bad today. I cannot go out. My rheumatism keeps me miserable."

This dear elderly lady got a lot of attention from her son, daughter, and the neighbors. She really wanted her rheumatism. She enjoyed her "misery" as she called it. This woman did not really want to be happy.

I suggested a curative procedure to her. I wrote down some biblical verses and told her that if she gave attention to these truths, her mental attitude would undoubtedly change and would result in her faith and confidence in being restored to health. She was not interested. There seems to be a peculiar, mental, morbid streak in many people, whereby they seem to enjoy being miserable and sad.

The truth is that happiness is a mental and spiritual state.

WHY CHOOSE UNHAPPINESS?

Many people choose unhappiness by entertaining these ideas:

"Today is a black day; everything is going to go wrong." "I am not going to succeed." "Everyone is against me." "Business is bad, and it is going to get worse." "I'm always late." "I never get the breaks." "He can, but I can't."

If you have this attitude of mind the first thing in the morning, you will attract all these experiences to you, and you will be very unhappy.

Begin to realize that the world you live in is determined largely by what goes on in your mind.

Marcus Aurelius, the great Roman philosopher and sage, said, "A man's life is what his thoughts make of it." Ralph Waldo Emerson, America's foremost philosopher, said, "A man is what he thinks all day long." The thoughts you habitually entertain in your mind have the tendency to actualize themselves in physical conditions.

Make certain you do not indulge in negative thoughts, defeatist thoughts, or unkind, depressing thoughts. Recall frequently to your mind that you can experience nothing outside your own mentality.

IF I HAD A MILLION DOLLARS, I WOULD BE HAPPY

I have visited many men in institutions who were millionaires but they insisted they were penniless and destitute. Some were incarcerated because of psychotic, paranoid, and manic-depressive tendencies. Wealth in and of itself will not make you happy. On the other hand, it is not a deterrent to happiness. Today, there are many people trying to buy happiness through the purchase of cellphones, television sets, automobiles, a home in the country, a private yacht, a swimming pool . . . but happiness cannot be purchased or procured in that way.

The kingdom of happiness is in your thought and feeling. Too many people have the idea that it takes something artificial to produce happiness.

Some say, "If I were elected mayor, made president of the organization, promoted to general manager of the corporation, I would be happy."

The truth is that happiness is a mental and spiritual state. None of these positions mentioned will necessarily bequeath happiness. Finding the law of divine order and right action lodged in your subconscious mind and applying these principles in all phases of your life are the source of your strength, joy, and happiness.

chapter three

Happiness Is the Harvest
of a Quiet Mind

While I was lecturing in San Francisco some years ago, I interviewed a man who was very unhappy and dejected over the way his business was going. He was the general manager. His heart was filled with resentment toward the vice president and the president of the organization. He claimed that they opposed him. Because of this internal strife, business was declining; he was receiving no dividends or stock bonuses.

This is how he solved his business problem: The first thing in the morning he affirmed quietly as follows:

"All those working in our corporation are honest, sincere, cooperative, faithful, and full of good will to all. They are mental and spiritual links in the chain of this corporation's growth, welfare, and prosperity. I radiate love, peace, and good will in my thoughts, words, and deeds to my two associates and to all those in the company. The president and the vice president of our company are divinely guided in all their undertakings. The infinite intelligence of my subconscious mind makes all decisions through me. There is only right action in all our business transactions and in our relationship with each other. I send the messengers of peace, love, and good will before me to the office. Peace and harmony reign supreme in the minds and hearts of all those in the company including myself. I now go forth into a new day, full of faith, confidence, and trust."

The business executive repeated this meditation slowly three times in the morning, feeling the truth of what he affirmed. When fearful or angry thoughts came into his mind during the day, he would say to himself, "Peace, harmony, and poise govern my mind at all times."

As he continued disciplining his mind in this manner, all the harmful thoughts ceased to come, and peace came into his mind. He reaped the harvest that comes with peace—happiness.

Subsequently, he wrote to me saying that at the end of about two weeks of reordering his mind, the president and the vice president called him into the office, praised his operations and his new constructive ideas, and remarked how fortunate they were to have him as general manager. He was very happy in discovering that one finds happiness within oneself.

THE BLOCK OR STUMP IS
NOT REALLY THERE

I read a newspaper article some years ago that told a story about a horse that had shied when he came to a stump on the road. Subsequently, every time the horse came to that same stump, he shied. The farmer dug the stump out, burned it, and leveled the old road. Yet, for twenty-five years, every time the horse passed the place where the former stump was, he shied. The horse was shying at the memory of a stump.

There is no block to your happiness save in your own thought life and mental imagery. Is fear or worry holding you back? Fear is a thought in your mind. You can dig it up this very moment by supplanting it with faith in success, achievement, and victory over all problems.

I knew a man who failed in business. He said to me, "I made mistakes. I've learned a lot. I am going back into business, and I will be a tremendous success." He faced up to that stump in his mind. He did not whine or complain; instead he tore up the stump of failure, and through believing in his inner powers to back him up, he banished all fear thoughts and old depressions. Believe in yourself, and you will succeed and be happy.

THE HAPPIEST PEOPLE

The happiest people are those who constantly bring forth and practice what is best in them. Happiness and virtue complement each other. The best are not only the happiest; the happiest are usually the best in the art of living life

The happiest people are those who constantly bring forth and practice what is best in them.

successfully. God is the highest and best in you. Express more of God's love, light, truth, and beauty, and you will become one of the happiest people in the world today.

Epictetus, the Greek stoic philosopher, said, "There is but one way to tranquility of mind and happiness; let this, therefore, be always ready at hand with thee, both when thou wakest early in the morning, and all the day long, and when thou goest late to sleep, to account no external things thine own, but commit all these to God."

chapter four

Happiness and Harmonious Human Relations

In studying this book, you learn that your subconscious mind is a recording machine, faithfully reproducing whatever you impress upon it. This is one of the reasons for the application of the Golden Rule in human relations. In this chapter we will consider several examples of "do unto others . . ."

Matthew 7:12 says, *All things whatsoever ye would that men should do unto you, do ye even so to them.*

This quotation has outer (conscious) and inner (subconscious) meanings. We are interested in its inner meaning from the standpoint of the subconscious mind, which is: As you would want others to think about you, you should think about them in like manner. As you would want others to feel about you, you should also feel about them in like manner. As you would want others to act toward you, you should act toward them in like manner.

For example, you may be polite and courteous to someone in your office but when his back is turned, you are very critical and resentful toward him in your mind. Such negative thoughts are highly destructive to you. It is like taking poison. You are actually taking mental poison; it will rob you of vitality, enthusiasm, strength, guidance, and good will. These negative thoughts and emotions sink down into your subconscious and cause all kinds of difficulties and maladies in your life.

THE MASTER KEY TO HAPPY RELATIONSHIPS WITH OTHERS

Judge not, that ye be not judged. For with what judgment ye judge, ye shall be judged, and with what measure ye mete, it shall be measured to you again. Matthew 7:1-2.

A study of these verses and the application of the inner truths therein contained represent the real key to harmonious relations. To judge is to think, to arrive at a mental verdict or conclusion in your mind. The thought you have about the other person is *your* thought because you are thinking it.

Your thoughts are creative; therefore, you actually create in your own experience what you think and feel about the other person. It is also true that the suggestion you give to another, you

Your thoughts are creative;
therefore, you actually create
in your own experience
what you think and feel.

also give to yourself because your mind is the creative medium.

This is why it is said, *For with what judgment ye judge, ye shall be judged.* When you know this law and the way your subconscious mind works, you are careful to think, feel, and act right toward the other. These verses teach you about the emancipation of mankind and reveal to you the solution to your individual problems.

DO UNTO OTHERS

The good you do for others comes back to you in like measure; the evil you do returns to you by the law of your own mind. If a man cheats and deceives another, he is actually cheating and deceiving himself. His sense of guilt and mood of loss inevitably will attract loss to him in some way, at some time. His subconscious records his mental act and reacts according to the mental intention or motivation.

Your subconscious mind is impersonal and unchanging, neither considering persons nor respecting religious affiliations or institutions of any kind. It is neither compassionate nor vindictive. The way you think, feel, and act toward others returns at last upon yourself.

BE AWARE OF YOURSELF

Begin now to observe yourself. Observe your reactions to people, conditions, and circumstances. How do you respond to the events and news of the day? It makes no difference if all the other people were wrong and you alone were right. If the news disturbs you, it is your evil because your negative emotions robbed you of peace and harmony.

A woman wrote me about her husband, saying that he goes into a rage when he reads what certain newspaper columnists write in the newspaper.

Negative emotions
rob you of peace
and harmony.

She added that this constant reaction of anger and suppressed rage on his part brought on bleeding ulcers, and his physician recommended an emotional reconditioning.

I invited this man to see me and I explained to him the way his mind functions, indicating how emotionally immature it was to get angry when others write articles with which he disapproves or disagrees.

He began to realize that he should give news writers freedom to express themselves even though they may disagree with him politically, religiously, or in any other way. In the same manner, the newspaper would give him freedom to write a letter to the editor expressing disagreement with the paper's published statements. This man learned that he could disagree without being disagreeable. He awakened to the simple truth that it is never what a person says or does that affects him; it is his *reaction* to what is said or done that matters.

This explanation was the cure for this man, and he realized that with a little practice he could master his morning tantrums. His wife told me, subsequently, that he laughed at himself and also at what the columnists say. They no longer have power to disturb, annoy, and irritate him. His ulcers have disappeared due to his emotional poise and serenity, and he is much happier.

BITTERNESS IS THE ENEMY
OF HAPPINESS

An executive assistant was very bitter toward some of the coworkers in her office because they were gossiping about her, and as she said, spreading vicious lies about her. She admitted that she did not like women. She said, "I hate women, but I like men." I discovered also that

"I am going to think, speak, and act from the principle of harmony, health, and peace within myself."

she spoke to the female employees who were under her supervision in a very haughty, imperious, and irritable tone of voice. She pointed out that they took delight in making things difficult for her. There was a certain pomposity in her way of speaking, and I could see where her tone of voice would affect some people unpleasantly.

If *all* the people in the office or factory annoy you, might there not be a common denominator? Isn't it a possibility that the vibration, annoyance, and turmoil may be due to some subconscious pattern or mental projection from *you?* We know that a dog will react ferociously if you hate or fear dogs. Animals pick up your subconscious vibrations and react accordingly. Human beings, on a subconscious level, are just as sensitive as dogs, cats, and other animals.

I suggested a process of prayer to this woman who hated women, explaining to her that when she began to identify herself with spiritual values and commenced to affirm the truths of life, her voice, mannerisms, and hatred of women would completely disappear. She was surprised to know that the emotion of hatred shows up in a person's speech, actions, writings, and in all phases of life. She established a pattern of prayer, which she practiced regularly, systematically, and conscientiously in the office. She ceased reacting in what had been her typical, resentful, and angry way.

The prayer was as follows: "I think, speak, and act lovingly, quietly, and peacefully. I now radiate love, peace, tolerance, and kindliness to all who criticized me and gossiped about me. I anchor my thoughts on peace, harmony, and good will to all. Whenever I am about to react negatively, I say firmly to myself, 'I am going to think, speak, and act from the standpoint of the principle of harmony, health, and peace within myself.'

"Creative intelligence leads, rules, and guides me in all my ways."

The practice of this prayer transformed her life, and she found that all criticism and annoyance ceased. Her coworkers became friends along life's journey. She discovered that she had no one to change but herself.

PROJECTING SELF-NEGATIVITY ONTO OTHERS

One day a salesman came to see me and described his difficulties in working with the sales manager of his organization. He had been with the company ten years and had received no promotion or recognition of any kind. He showed me his sales figures, which were greater proportionately than the other salespeople in the territory. He said that the sales manager did not like him, that he was unjustly treated, and that at conferences the manager was rude to him, and at times ridiculed his suggestions.

I explained that undoubtedly the cause was to a great degree within himself, and that his mental concept and belief about his superior bore witness to this in the way his superior *reacted* to him. "The measure we mete, shall be measured to us again" [Matthew 7:2]. His mental measure or concept of the sales manager was that he was mean and cantankerous. He was filled with bitterness and hostility toward the executive. On his way to work he conducted a vigorous conversation with himself filled with criticism, mental arguments, recriminations, and denunciations of his sales manager.

What he gave out mentally he was inevitably bound to get back. I helped this salesman realize that his inner speech was highly destructive because of the intensity and force of his silent thoughts and emotions, so much so that he personally conducted mental condemnation and vilification of the sales manager back into his own subconscious mind. This brought about the negative response from his boss as well as creating many other personal, physical, and emotional disorders.

He began to pray frequently as follows:

"I am the only thinker in my universe. I am responsible for what I think about my boss. My sales manager is not responsible for the way I think about him. I refuse to give power to any person, place, or thing to annoy me or disturb me. I wish health, success, peace of mind, and happiness for my boss. I sincerely wish him well, and I know he is divinely guided in all his ways."

He repeated this prayer out loud slowly, quietly, and feelingly, knowing that his mind is like a garden, and that whatever he planted in the garden would come forth like seeds after their kind.

I also taught him to practice mental imagery prior to sleep in this way: He imagined that his sales manager was congratulating him on his fine work, on his zeal and enthusiasm, and on his wonderful response from customers. He felt the reality of all this, felt his handshake, heard the tone of his voice, and saw his boss smile. He made a real mental movie, dramatizing it to the best of his ability.

Night after night he conducted this mental movie, knowing that his subconscious mind was the receptive plate on which his conscious imagery would be impressed.

When you become
emotionally mature,
you do not respond
negatively to the
criticism and
resentment of others.

Gradually, by a process of what may be termed mental and spiritual osmosis, the impression was made on his subconscious mind and the expression automatically came forth. His boss subsequently called him up to San Francisco, congratulated him, and gave him a new assignment as Division Sales Manager with the responsibility for more than one hundred employees, and a big salary increase. The salesman changed his concept and estimate of his boss, and the latter responded accordingly.

BECOMING EMOTIONALLY MATURE

What other people say or do cannot really annoy or irritate you unless you permit them to disturb you. The only way others can annoy you is through your own thought. For example, if you get angry, you have to go through the following four stages in your mind:

1. You begin to think about what has been said.

2. You decide to get angry.

3. You generate an emotion of rage.

3. Then, you decide to act. Perhaps, you talk back and react in kind.

You can see that the thought, emotion, reaction, and action all take place in your mind.

When you become emotionally mature, you do not respond negatively to the criticism and resentment of others. To do so would mean that you have descended to that state of low mental vibration and become one with the negative atmosphere of the other. Identify yourself with your aim in life, and do not permit any person, place, or thing to deflect you from your inner sense of peace, tranquility, and happiness.

THE MEANING OF LOVE IN HARMONIOUS
HUMAN RELATIONS

Sigmund Freud, the Austrian founder of psychoanalysis, said that unless the personality has love, it sickens and dies. Love includes understanding, good will, and respect for the divinity in the other person. The more love and good will you emanate and exude, the more they come back to you.

If you puncture the other person's ego and wound his estimate of himself, you cannot gain his good will. Recognize that everyone wants to be loved and appreciated and made to feel important in the world.

Realize that the other person is conscious of his true worth, and that, like yourself, he feels the dignity of being an expression of the One Life Principle animating all. As you do this consciously and knowingly, you build the other

Recognize that
everyone wants to be
loved and appreciated
and made to feel
important in the world.

person up, and that person will return your love and good will.

HE HATED AUDIENCES

An actor told me that the audience booed and hissed at him during his first appearance on the stage. He added that the play was badly written and that undoubtedly he did not play a good role. He admitted openly to me that for months afterward he hated audiences. He called them dopes, dummies, stupid, ignorant, gullible, etc. He quit his acting career in disgust and went to work in a drugstore for a year.

One day a friend invited him into the city to hear a lecture on "How to Get Along With Ourselves." This lecture changed his life.

He went back to the stage and began to pray sincerely for the audience and himself. He poured out love and good will every night before appearing on the stage. He made it a habit to claim that the peace of God filled the hearts of all those present, and that all present were lifted up and inspired. During each performance he sent out love vibrations to the audience. Today he is a great actor and he loves and respects people. His good will and esteem are transmitted to others and are felt by them.

HANDLING DIFFICULT PEOPLE

There are difficult people in the world who are twisted and distorted mentally. They are malconditioned. Many are argumentative, uncooperative, cantankerous, cynical, and sour on life.

These individuals are sick psychologically. Many people have deformed and distorted minds, perhaps suffering from a diagnosed or undiagnosed mental illness. Many people are bitter because of physical limitations. You would not condemn a person who had high blood pressure; nor should you condemn anyone with a difficult personality. You should have compassion and understanding.

To understand all is to forgive all.

MISERY LOVES COMPANY

A hateful, frustrated, distorted, and twisted personality is out of tune with the Infinite, and resents those who are peaceful, happy, and joyous.

Usually miserable people criticize, condemn, and vilify those who have been very good and kind to them. Their attitude is this: "Why should others be so happy when I am so miserable?" Misery wants to drag others down to its own level. Misery loves company. When you understand this you remain unmoved, calm, and dispassionate.

THE PRACTICE OF EMPATHY IN
HUMAN RELATIONS

A man visited me recently and told me that he hated a female coworker in his office. His reason was that the other person was better looking, happier, and wealthier than he, and, in addition, was engaged to the boss of the company where they worked. One day, after the marriage had taken place, the hated coworker came into the office with a child. The child put her arms around her mother and said, "Mommy, Mommy, I love my new daddy! Look what he gave me!" The child showed her mother a wonderful new toy.

This man, having witnessed this, said to me, "My heart went out to that little girl, and I knew how happy she must feel. I suddenly got a vision of how happy my coworker was, and I felt warmth and happiness for her. I went into

Remain true to
your ideal.

the office and wished her all the happiness in the world, and I meant it."

In psychological circles today, this is called empathy, which simply means the imaginative projection of your mental attitude onto another person.

This man projected his mental mood—or the feeling of his heart—onto his coworker, and began to think and look at the world through the other woman's brain. He actually began thinking and feeling *as* the coworker and also as the child, because he likewise had projected himself into the mind of the child. And through the child's mental/emotional eyes, he was looking out from that vantage point onto his coworker.

If tempted to injure or think ill of another, project yourself mentally into the mind of

Harmony of the part is the harmony of the whole.

Moses and think from the standpoint of the Ten Commandments. If you are prone to be envious, jealous, or angry, project yourself into the mind of Jesus, Buddha, Mohammed, and think from that standpoint, and you will feel the truth of the words *Love ye one another.*

APPEASEMENT NEVER WINS

Allow yourself empathy, allow yourself to step into another's shoes and see through their eyes. However, do not permit people to take advantage of you and gain their way through temper tantrums or crying jags. Do not allow them to project their subconscious detritus onto you. These people are dictators who try to enslave you and make you do their bidding. Be firm but kind, and refuse to yield. Empathy and understanding are not the same as appeasement. Appeasement never wins. Refuse to contribute to their delinquency, selfishness, and possessiveness. Remember, do that which is right. You are here to fulfill your ideal and remain true to the eternal truth and spiritual values of life.

Give no one the power to deflect you from your life's goal, which is to express your hidden talents to the world, to serve humanity, and to reveal more and more of God's wisdom, truth, and beauty to all.

Remain true to your ideal. Know definitely and absolutely that whatever contributes to your peace, happiness, and fulfillment must of necessity bless all who walk the earth.

The harmony of the part is the harmony of the whole, for the whole is in the part, and the part is in the whole. As Paul says, all you owe others is love, and love is the fulfilling of the law of happiness and peace of mind.

chapter five

Forgiveness as a Path to Happiness

Life plays no favorites. God is Life, and this Life Principle is flowing through you at this moment. God loves to express Himself as harmony, peace, beauty, joy, and abundance through you. This is called the will of God or the tendency of Life.

If you set up resistance in your mind to the flow of Life through you, this emotional congestion will get snarled up in your subconscious mind and cause all kinds of negative conditions. God has nothing to do with unhappy or chaotic conditions in the world. Our own negative and destructive thinking brings about all these conditions. Therefore, it is silly to blame God for our trouble, sickness, and unhappiness.

Many of us habitually set up mental resistance to the flow of Life by accusing and reproaching God for the suffering of mankind. Others cast the blame on God for their pains, aches, loss, personal tragedies, and accidents. They are angry at God and they believe He is responsible for their misery.

As long as people entertain such negative concepts about God they will experience the automatic negative reactions from their subconscious minds.

Actually, such people who outwardly blame do not know that they are only punishing themselves. They cannot go forward into happiness and creative activity unless they see the truth, find release, and give up all condemnation, resentment, and anger against anyone or any power outside themselves. The minute these people entertain a God of love in their minds and hearts, and when they believe that God lovingly watches over them, cares for them, guides them, sustains and strengthens them, then this concept and belief about God—the Life Principle—will be accepted by their subconscious mind, and they will find themselves blessed in countless ways.

LIFE ALWAYS FORGIVES YOU

Life forgives you when you cut your finger. The subconscious intelligence within you sets about immediately to repair it. New cells build bridges over the cut. Should you eat some spoiled food by error, Life forgives you and causes you to regurgitate it in order to preserve you. If you burn your hand, the Life Principle reduces the edema and congestion, and gives you new skin, tissue, and cells. Life holds no grudges against you—it is *always* forgiving you. Life brings you back to happiness, vitality, harmony, and peace if you cooperate by thinking in harmony with nature. Negative, hurtful memories, bitterness, and ill will clutter up and impede the free flow of the Life Principle in you.

BANISH THAT FEELING OF GUILT

I knew a man who worked every night until one o'clock in the morning. He paid no attention to his two boys or his wife. He was always too busy working hard. He thought people should pat him on the back because he was working so arduously and persistently past midnight every night. He had sky-rocketing blood pressure and was full of guilt.

Unconsciously, he was punishing himself through his hard work and the way in which he

Life brings you back
to happiness if you
think in harmony
with nature.

was completely ignoring his children. A happy father does not do that. He is interested in his boys and in their development. A happy spouse does not shut his wife out of his world.

I explained to him why he was working so arduously: "There is something eating you inside, otherwise, you would not act this way. You are punishing yourself, and you have to learn to forgive yourself."

As it turned out, he did have a deep sense of guilt. It was guilt over a brother.

I explained to him that God was not punishing him but that he was punishing himself.

Look at it this way: if you misuse the laws of life, you will suffer accordingly. If you put your hand on a naked charged wire, you will get burned. The forces of nature are not evil; it is your use of them that determines whether they have a good or evil effect. Electricity is not evil; it depends on how you use it, whether to burn down a structure or light up a home. The only sin is ignorance of the law, and the only punishment is the automatic reaction of your misuse of the law.

If you misuse the principle of chemistry, you may blow up your home or office or factory. If you strike your hand on a board, you may cause your hand to bleed. The board is not for that purpose. Its purpose may be to lean upon or to support your feet.

This man realized that God does not condemn or punish anyone, and that all his suffering was due to the reaction of his subconscious mind to his own negative and destructive thinking. He had cheated his brother at one time, and the brother had now passed on. He was full of remorse and guilt.

I asked him, "Would you cheat your brother now?" He said, "No."

"Did you feel you were justified at the time?"
He replied, "Yes."

"But, you would not do it now?"

He added, "No, I am helping others to know how to live."

I added the following comment, "You have a greater reason and understanding now. Forgiveness is to forgive yourself. Forgiveness is getting your thoughts in line with the divine law of harmony. Self-condemnation is called hell (bondage and restriction); forgiveness is called heaven (harmony and peace)."

The burden of guilt and self-condemnation was lifted from his mind, and he returned to a state of happiness and peace. He stopped avoiding his family. His blood pressure returned to normal. Understanding his subconscious mind was the cure.

CRITICISM CANNOT HURT YOU
WITHOUT YOUR CONSENT

A schoolteacher told me that one of her associates criticized a speech she had given, saying to her that she spoke too fast, she swallowed some of her words, she couldn't be heard, her diction was poor, and her speech ineffective. She was furious and full of resentment toward her critic.

She admitted to me, however, that the criticism was just. Her initial reaction was really childish, and she agreed that the feedback was really a blessing and a marvelous corrective. She proceeded immediately to supplement her deficiencies in her speech by enrolling in a course in public speaking. She wrote and thanked her critic for taking an interest in her, expressing appreciation for her conclusions and findings, which enabled the teacher to correct the matter at once.

But suppose none of the things mentioned by her critic had been true of the teacher. The latter would have realized that her class material had upset the prejudices, superstitions, or narrow sectarian beliefs of the critic, and that the other person was simply pouring forth her resentment because a psychological boil had been hurt.

This type of understanding is what it means to be compassionate. The next logical step would be to pray for the other person's peace, harmony, and understanding.

You cannot be hurt when you know that you are master of your thoughts, reactions, and emotions.

Emotions follow thoughts, and you have the power to reject all thoughts, which may disturb or upset you.

Some years ago I visited a church to perform a marriage ceremony. The groom did not appear, and at the end of two hours, the bride-to-be shed a few tears, and then said to me, "I prayed for divine guidance. This might be the answer for He never faileth."

That was her reaction—faith in God and all things good. She had no bitterness in her heart because as she said, "It must not have been right action because my prayer was for right action for both of us." Someone else having a similar experience would have gone into a tantrum, had an emotional fit, required sedation, or become horribly enraged.

Tune in to the infinite intelligence within your subconscious depths, and trust the answer in the same way that you would trust a parent holding you close as a child.

This is how you can acquire poise and mental and emotional health.

FORGIVENESS IS NECESSARY
FOR HEALING

Forgiveness of others is essential to mental peace. You must forgive everyone who has ever hurt you if you want to find happiness. Forgive yourself by getting your thoughts in harmony with divine law and order. You cannot really forgive yourself completely until you have forgiven others first. To refuse to forgive yourself is nothing more or less than spiritual pride or ignorance.

In the psychosomatic field of medicine today, it is being constantly stressed that resentment, condemnation of others, remorse, and hostility are behind a host of maladies ranging from headaches to cardiac disease. Many people who suffer physically have been hurt,

Emotion follows
thought, and you have
the power to reject all
thoughts that may
upset you.

mistreated, deceived, or injured, and are full of resentment and hatred for those who hurt them. This holding onto to hurt will inflame and fester wounds in your subconscious mind. There is only one remedy. You must cut out and discard the hurts and the perceived wrong, and the one and only sure way to do this is through forgiveness.

FORGIVENESS IS LOVE IN ACTION

The essential ingredient in the art of forgiveness is the willingness to forgive. If you sincerely desire to forgive the other, you are 51 percent over the hurdle. I feel sure you know that to forgive someone does not necessarily mean that you like the other person or want to associate with them. You cannot be compelled to like someone, neither can a government legislate good will, love, peace, or tolerance. It is quite impossible to like people because someone in Washington issues an edict to that effect. We can, however, love people without liking them.

The Bible says, *Love ye one another.* This is something anyone can do who really wants to do it. Love means that you wish upon another person health, happiness, peace, joy, and all the blessings of life. There is only one prerequisite and that is sincerity. You are not being magnanimous when you forgive; you are really being selfish, because what you wish for the other, you are actually wishing for yourself. The reason is that you are thinking it and you are feeling it. As you think and feel, so are you. Could anything be simpler than that?

TECHNIQUE OF FORGIVENESS

The following is a simple method that works wonders in your life as you practice it:

Quiet your mind, relax, and let go. Think of God and His love for you, and then affirm, "I fully and freely forgive (mention the name of the offender); I release him/her mentally and spiritually. I completely forgive everything connected with the matter in question. I am free, and he/she is free. It is a marvelous feeling. It is my day of general amnesty. I release anybody and everybody who has ever hurt me, and I wish for each and everyone health, happiness, peace, and all the blessings of life. I do this freely, joyously, and lovingly, and whenever I think of the person or persons who hurt me, I say, 'I have released you, and all the blessings of life are yours.' I am free and you are free. It is wonderful!"

The great secret of true forgiveness is that once you have forgiven the person, it is unnecessary to repeat the prayer. Whenever the person comes to your mind or the particular hurt happens to enter your mind, wish the delinquent well and say, "Peace be unto you." Do this as often as the thought enters your mind. You will find that after a few days the thought of the person or experience will return less and less often, until it fades into nothingness.

THE ACID TEST FOR FORGIVENESS

There is an acid test for gold. There is also an acid test for forgiveness. If I should tell you something wonderful about someone who has wronged you, cheated you, or defrauded you, and you sizzled at hearing the good news about this person, the roots of hatred would still be in your subconscious mind, playing havoc with you. That is the acid test.

Let us suppose you had a painful abscess on your jaw a year ago and you told me about it. I would casually ask you if you had any pain

When you
understand the
creative law of your
own mind, you cease
to blame others
for your unhappiness.

now. You would probably say, "Of course not, I have a memory of it but no pain." That is the whole story. You may have a memory of the incident but no sting or hurt anymore. This is the acid test, and you must meet it psychologically and spiritually, otherwise, you are simply deceiving yourself and not practicing the true art of forgiveness.

To *forgive* is to *give* something *for.* Give love, peace, joy, wisdom, and all the blessings of life to others, until there is no sting left in your mind.

TO UNDERSTAND ALL
IS TO FORGIVE ALL

When you understand the creative law of your own mind, you cease to blame other people or conditions for making or marring your life. You knows that your own thoughts and feelings create your destiny. Furthermore, you are aware

that externals are not the causes and condition-
ers of your life and your experiences.

To think that others can mar your happiness,
that you are the football of a cruel fate, that you
must oppose and fight others for a living—all
these and other thoughts like them are unten-
able when you understand that *thoughts are things.*
The Bible says it this way: *For as a man thinketh in
his heart, so is he.* Proverbs 23:7.

chapter six

Steps to Attracting Happiness

True and lasting happiness will come into your life the day you get the clear realization that the power of your subconscious mind can clear the roadblocks to achieving it. The stories and lessons in this book have focused on three simple concepts: 1) the power of prayer and intention, 2) doing unto others as you would have them do unto you, 3) the profound act of forgiveness.

Here is a summary of the steps to attracting happiness in your life.

THE POWER OF YOUR SUBCONSCIOUS MIND

- William James said that the greatest discovery of the 19th century was the power of the subconscious mind touched by faith.

- There is tremendous power within you. Happiness will come to you when you acquire a sublime confidence in this power. Then you will make your dreams come true.

- You can rise victorious over any defeat and realize the cherished desires of your heart through the marvelous power of your subconscious mind. This is the meaning of *whosoever trusteth in the Lord [spiritual laws of the subconscious mind], happy is he.*

You must
choose happiness.
Happiness is a habit.

- You must *choose* happiness. Happiness is a habit. It is a good habit to ponder often on *Whatsoever things are true, whatsoever things are honest, whatsoever things are just, whatsoever things are pure, whatsoever things are lovely, whatsoever things are of good report; if there be any virtue, and if there be any praise, think on these things.* Philippians 4:8.

- When you open your eyes in the morning, say to yourself, I choose happiness today. I choose success today. I choose right action today. I choose love and good will for all today. I choose peace today. Pour life, love, and interest into this affirmation, and you have chosen happiness.

- Give thanks for all your blessings several times a day. Pray for the peace, happiness, and prosperity of all members of your family, your associates, and all people everywhere.

- You must sincerely desire to be happy. Nothing is accomplished without desire. Desire is a wish with wings of imagination and faith. Imagine the fulfillment of your desire, and feel its reality, and it will come to pass. Happiness comes in answered prayer.

- By constantly dwelling on thoughts of fear, worry, anger, hate, and failure, you will become very depressed and unhappy. Remember, your life is what your thoughts make of it.

- You cannot buy happiness. Some millionaires are very happy, some are very unhappy. Many people with few worldly goods are very happy, and some are very unhappy. Some married people are happy, and some very unhappy. Some single people are happy, and some are very unhappy. The kingdom of happiness is in your thought and feeling.

You cannot buy
happiness. The kingdom
of happiness is in your
thought and feeling.

- Happiness is the harvest of a quiet mind. Anchor your thoughts on peace, poise, security, and divine guidance, and your mind will be productive of happiness.

- There is no block to your happiness. External things are not causative; these are effects, not cause. Take your cue from the only creative principle within you. Your thought is cause, and a new cause produces a new effect. Choose happiness.

- The happiest man is he who brings forth the highest and the best in him. God is the highest and the best in him, for the kingdom of God is within.

HAPPY HUMAN RELATIONS

- Your subconscious mind is a recording machine, which reproduces your habitual thinking.

Think good of the other, and you are actually thinking good about yourself.

- A hateful or resentful thought is a mental poison. Do not think ill of another for to do so is to think ill of yourself. You are the only thinker in your universe, and your thoughts are creative.

- Your mind is a creative medium; therefore, what you think and feel about the other, you are bringing to pass in your own experience. This is the psychological meaning of the Golden Rule. As you would want someone to think about you, think about that person in the same manner.

- To cheat, rob, or defraud another brings lack, loss, and limitation to yourself. Your subconscious mind records your inner motivations, thoughts, and feelings. These being of a negative nature—loss, limitation, and trouble—come to you in countless ways. Actually, what you do to another, you are doing to yourself.

- The good you do, the kindness proffered, the love and good will you send forth, will all come back to you multiplied in many ways.

- You are the only thinker in your world. You are responsible for the way you think about others. Remember, the other person is not responsible for the way you think about them. Your thoughts are reproduced. What are you thinking now?

- Become emotionally mature and permit other people to differ from you. They have a perfect right to disagree with you, and you have the same freedom to disagree with them. You can disagree without being disagreeable.

- Animals pick up your fear vibrations and snap at you. If you love animals, they will never attack you. Human beings are just as sensitive as dogs, cats, and other animals.

- Your inner speech, representing your silent thoughts and feelings, is reflected in the reactions of others toward you.

- Wish for the other what you wish for yourself. This is the key to harmonious human relations.

- Change your concept and estimate of those around you. Feel and know that they are practicing the Golden Rule and the Law of Love, and they will respond accordingly.

- Another person cannot annoy you or irritate you without your permission. Your thought is creative; you can bless others. If someone calls you a skunk, you have the freedom to respond, "God's peace fills your soul."

- Love is the answer to getting along with others. Love is understanding, good will, and respecting the divinity of the other.

- Have compassion and understanding for others. To understand all is to forgive all.

- Rejoice in the success, promotion, and good fortune of others. In doing so, you attract good fortune to yourself.

- Never yield to emotional scenes and tantrums of others. Appeasement never wins. Do not be a doormat. Adhere to that which is right. Stick to your ideal, knowing that the mental outlook, which gives you peace, happiness, and joy, is right, good, and true. What blesses you, blesses all.

- All you owe any person in the world is love, and love is wishing for everyone what you wish for yourself—health, happiness, and all the blessings of life.

FORGIVENESS

- God, or Life Principle, plays no favorites. Life, or God, favors you when you align yourself with the principle of harmony, health, joy, and peace.

- God, or Life Principle, never sends disease, sickness, accident, or suffering. We bring these things on ourselves by our own negative destructive thinking based upon the law "As we sow, so shall we reap."

- Your *concept* of God is the most important thing. If you really believe in a God of love, your subconscious mind will respond in countless blessings to you. Believe in a God of love.

- Life Principle, or God, holds no grudge against you. Life never condemns you. Life heals a severe cut on your hand. Life forgives you if you burn your finger. It reduces the edema and restores the part to wholeness and perfection.

- Your guilt complex is a false concept of God and Life. God, or Life Principle, does not punish or judge you. You do this to yourself by your false beliefs, negative thinking, and self-condemnation.

- God, or Life Principle, does not condemn or punish you. The forces of nature are not evil. The effect of their use depends on how you use the power within you. You can use electricity to kill someone or to light the house.

- You can use water to drown a child, or quench his thirst. Good and evil come right back to the thought and creative purpose in your own mind.

- God, or Life Principle, never punishes. We punishes ourselves through our false concepts of God, Life, and the Universe. Our thoughts are creative, and we create our own misery.

- If someone criticizes you, and these faults are within you, rejoice, give thanks, and appreciate the comments. This gives you the opportunity to correct the particular fault.

- You cannot be hurt by criticism when you know that you are master of your thoughts, reactions, and emotions. This gives you the opportunity to pray and bless the other, thereby blessing yourself.

- When you pray for guidance and right action, take what comes. Realize it is good and very good. Then there is no cause for self-pity, criticism, or hatred.

- There is nothing good or bad, but thinking makes it so. There is no evil in sex, the desire for food, wealth, or true expression. It depends on how you use these urges, desires, or aspirations. Your desire for food can be met without killing someone for a loaf of bread.

- Resentment, hatred, ill will, and hostility are behind a host of maladies. Forgive yourself and everybody else by pouring out love, life, joy, and good will to all those who have hurt you. Continue until such time as you meet them in your mind and you are at peace with them.

- To forgive is to *give* something *for*. Give love, peace, joy, wisdom, and all the blessings of life to the other, until there is no sting left in your mind. This is really the acid test of forgiveness.

- Let the past be the past. If someone in the past has hurt you, lied about you, vilified you, and said all manner of evil about you, is your thought of that person *still* negative? Do you sizzle when he or she comes into your mind? If so, the roots of hatred are still there, playing havoc with you and your good. The only way is to wither them with love by wishing for the person all the blessings of life, until you can meet the person in your mind, and you can sincerely react with a benediction of peace and good will. This is the meaning of *Forgive until seventy times seven.*

The good you do, the
kindness proffered,
the love you send forth,
will all come back to you
multiplied in many ways.

About the Author

Dr. Joseph Murphy (1898–1981) was a leading proponent of the New Thought movement, which developed in the late 19th and early 20th centuries by philosophers and deep thinkers who advocated and practiced a new way of looking at life and obtaining desires. Acclaimed as a major figure in the human potential movement, Murphy has been seen as the spiritual heir to writers like Napoleon Hill, Dale Carnegie, and Emmet Fox, and had a direct influence on contemporary motivational writers such as Tony Robbins and Louise Hay.

Schooled in the Jesuit tradition, Murphy became increasingly interested in new experiences through the power of prayer, and eventually his studies turned his interest toward various Asian religions and Eastern philosophy. He went to India to pursue indepth study of all of the major faiths from the time of their beginning, and extended these studies to the great philosophers from ancient times until the present.

Murphy wrote more than thirty books, the most famous of which, *The Power of Your Subconscious Mind*, first published in 1963, became an international bestseller, with millions of copies sold worldwide. In the mid 1940s, he moved to Los Angeles, where he became minister of the Los Angeles Divine Science Church, which he built into one of the largest New Thought congregations in the country.

HAMPTON ROADS
PUBLISHING COMPANY

. . . for the evolving human spirit

Hampton Roads Publishing Company publishes
books on a variety of subjects, including spiritu-
ality, health, and other related topics.

For a copy of our latest trade catalog, call
(978) 465-0504 or visit our distributor's website
at *www.redwheelweiser.com*, where you can also sign
up for our newsletter and special offers.